INSIDE THE VOLCANO

MICHAEL BENSON'S STORY

BY BLAKE HOENA

COVER ILLUSTRATION BY TATE YOTTER
INTERIOR ILLUSTRATION BY ALEXANDRA CONKINS
COLOR BY GERARDO SANDOVAL

BELLWETHER MEDIA • MINNEAPOLIS, MN

STRAY FROM REGULAR READS
WITH BLACK SHEEP BOOKS.
FEEL A RUSH WITH EVERY READ!

This edition first published in 2022 by Bellwether Media, Inc.

No part of this publication may be reproduced in whole or in part without written permission of the publisher.
For information regarding permission, write to Bellwether Media, Inc., Attention: Permissions Department,
6012 Blue Circle Drive, Minnetonka, MN 55343.

Library of Congress Cataloging-in-Publication Data

LC record for Inside the Volcano: Michael Benson's Story available at https://lccn.loc.gov/2021025034

Text copyright © 2022 by Bellwether Media, Inc. BLACK SHEEP and associated logos are trademarks
and/or registered trademarks of Bellwether Media, Inc.

Editor: Betsy Rathburn   Designer: Andrea Schneider

Printed in the United States of America, North Mankato, MN.

TABLE OF CONTENTS

Red text identifies historical quotes.

INTO THE KĪLAUEA VOLCANO

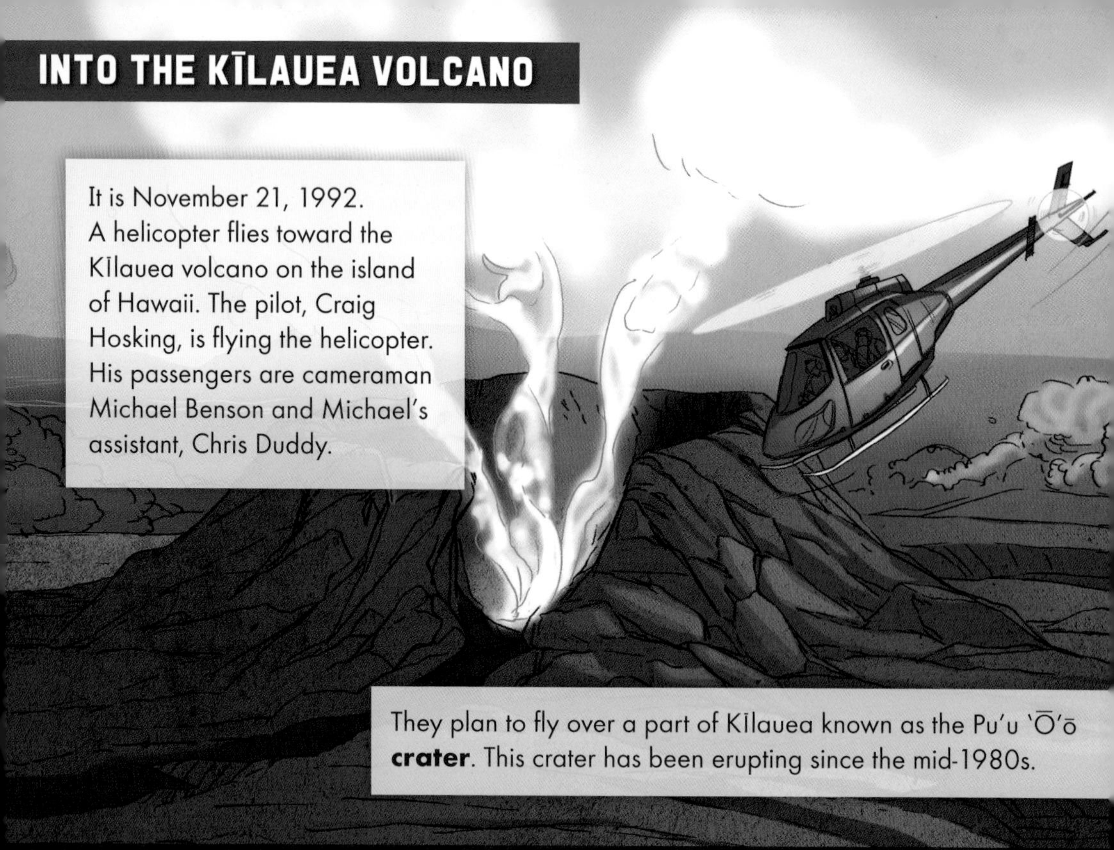
It is November 21, 1992. A helicopter flies toward the Kīlauea volcano on the island of Hawaii. The pilot, Craig Hosking, is flying the helicopter. His passengers are cameraman Michael Benson and Michael's assistant, Chris Duddy.
They plan to fly over a part of Kīlauea known as the Pu'u 'Ō'ō **crater**. This crater has been erupting since the mid-1980s.

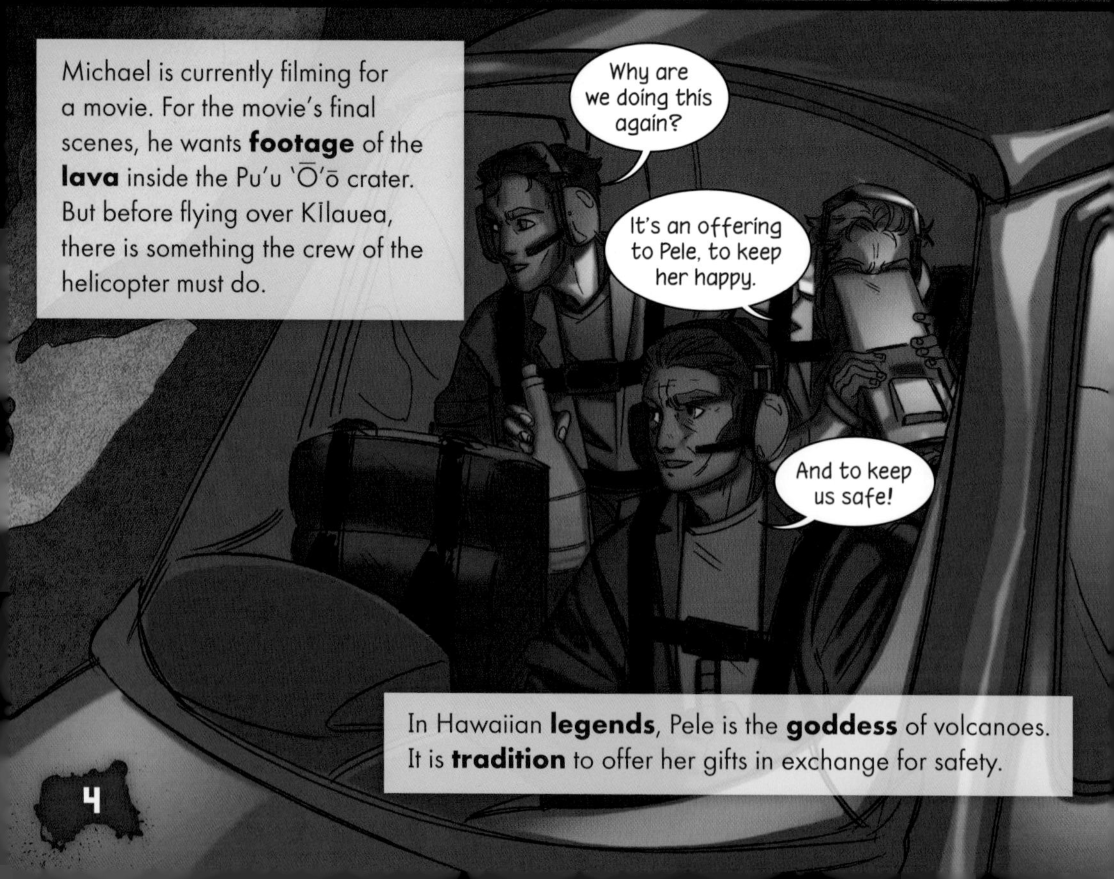
Michael is currently filming for a movie. For the movie's final scenes, he wants **footage** of the **lava** inside the Pu'u 'Ō'ō crater. But before flying over Kīlauea, there is something the crew of the helicopter must do.
Why are we doing this again?
It's an offering to Pele, to keep her happy.
And to keep us safe!
In Hawaiian **legends**, Pele is the **goddess** of volcanoes. It is **tradition** to offer her gifts in exchange for safety.

People believe the offering keeps Pele from getting angry. Then they are able to safely enter her home on Kīlauea.

Here it goes!

But the strong winds ruin Chris's throw.

I can't believe you missed. The volcano is 2 miles wide!

Let's just hope Pele doesn't get angry with us.

PLAY ▶
REC
VHS

Despite their failed offering, Michael and his crew get to work shooting footage of the bubbling lava below.

AM 10:25
NOV.21 .1992

00:00:45:04

5

After the first attempt, Michael reviews the footage. But he is not happy with it. He decides to try filming the lava again.

Craig, can we try that one again? Let's get a little closer this time.

Sure thing.

Michael begins to shoot more footage.

But soon after entering the crater...

What's happening?

I think we're losing power.

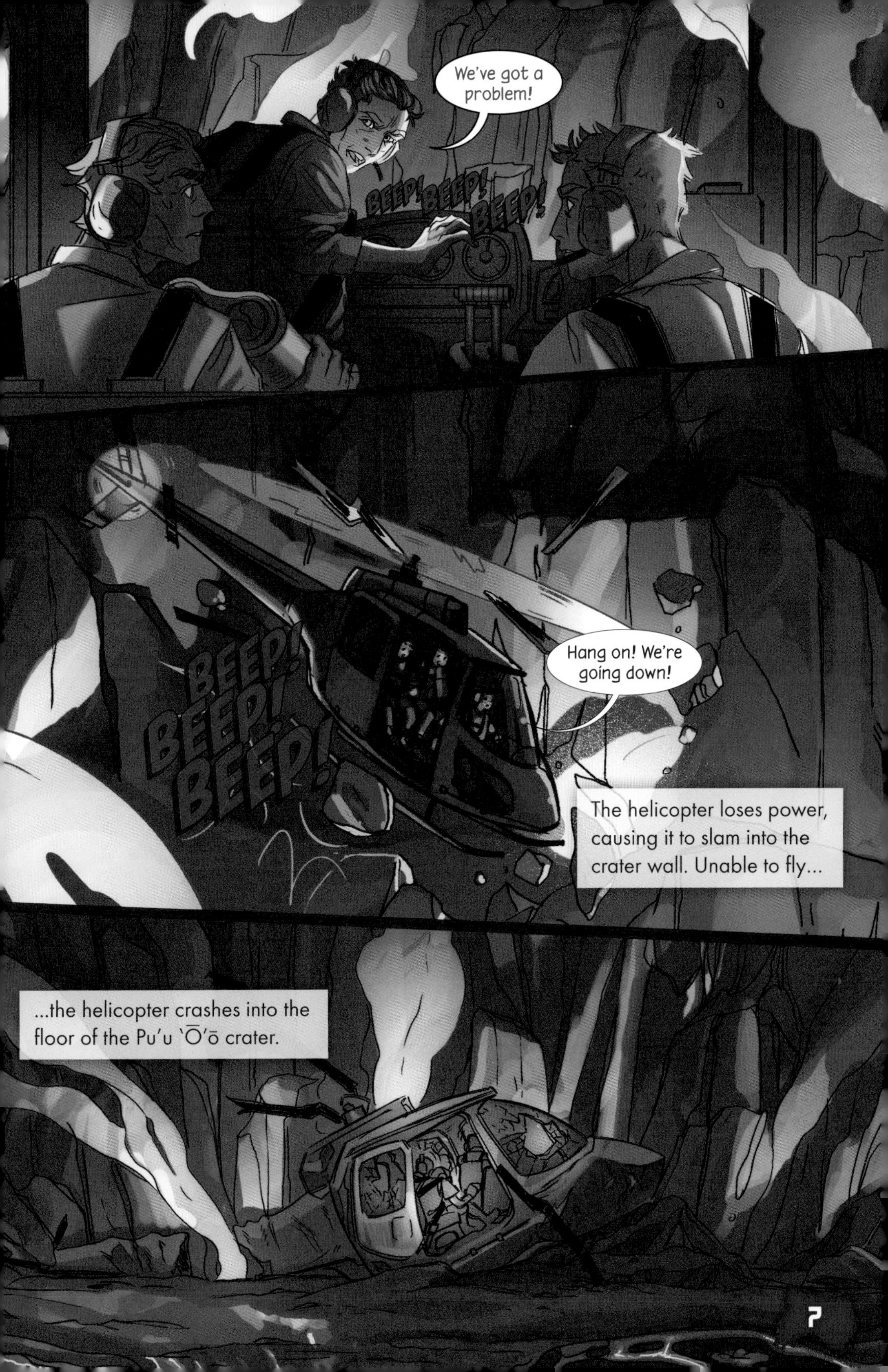

We've got a problem!
BEEP! BEEP! BEEP!
BEEP! BEEP! BEEP!
Hang on! We're going down!
The helicopter loses power, causing it to slam into the crater wall. Unable to fly...
...the helicopter crashes into the floor of the Pu'u 'Ō'ō crater.

INSIDE THE CRATER

The helicopter crashes about 150 feet below the rim of the crater. It is not far from a pool of **molten** lava.

We're lucky—

—to be alive.

But the three men are far from safe. The **fumes** inside the crater are **toxic**. They make it difficult to breathe.

As the men catch their breaths, they try to figure out where they are.

You two okay?

I think I'm okay.

Where are we?

At the bottom of the crater.

We can't survive for long down here.

What are we going to do?

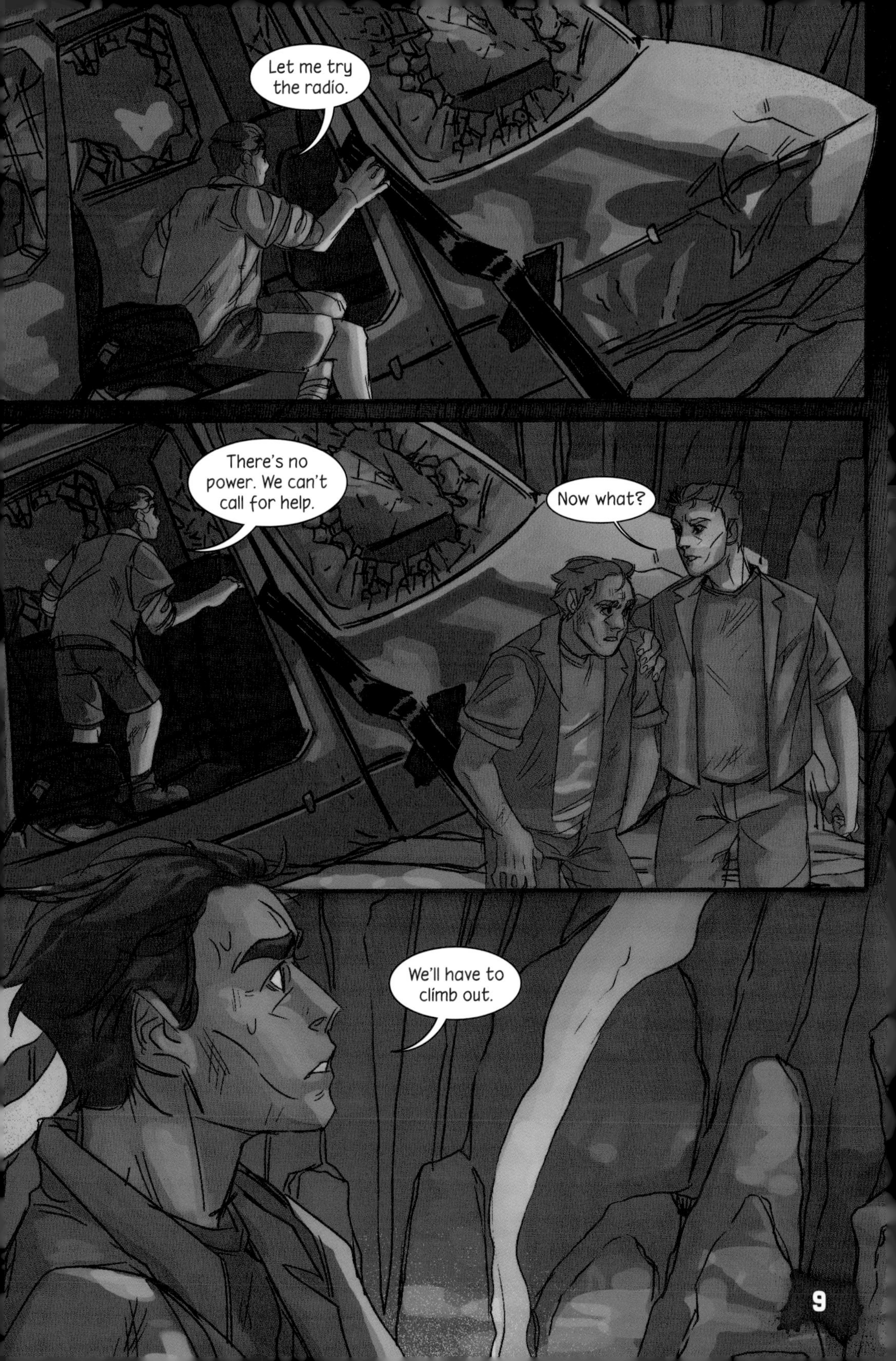
Let me try the radio.
There's no power. We can't call for help.
Now what?
We'll have to climb out.

The three men begin the climb up the crater wall. The volcanic rock is as sharp as glass. But that is not the only problem the men face.

As they make their way up, the walls of the crater get steeper...

...and their climb more **treacherous**.

AHHH!

You okay up there, Chris?

Yeah, but I don't think I can go any farther.

Unable to climb any higher, the men must figure out another way to survive.

Climbing up is not going to work.

We have no choice.

I'll go back down. Maybe I can fix the radio.

Maybe this camera battery can power the radio.

Craig manages to climb back down to the helicopter. Michael and Chris are not sure if he will return.

But after a while, they hear a voice calling below them.

I got a **mayday** out!

We're saved!

Craig fixes the radio and sends out a message about the crash. But the men are not out of danger yet.

After spending too much time in the toxic fumes at the bottom of the crater, Craig is in extreme danger. He is too weak to climb back to Michael and Chris. He tries to warn them to stay on the wall, but his lungs feel like they are on fire.

COUGH!

Don't come down here. The air—

—I can't breathe.

The conditions grow worse and worse. Soon, Craig stops answering.

Craig! Answer me! Are you okay down there?

They begin to wonder if their friend is still safe.

Then, Michael and Chris hear the sound of a helicopter.

CHOP! CHOP! CHOP!

Here! I'm right here!

But the helicopter does not see the two men. Michael and Chris listen as its noise slowly fades away.

CHOP! CHOP! CHOP!

Why is it leaving? Can't they see us?

The two men do not realize that the helicopter managed to rescue Craig. They begin to worry that it is the last rescue helicopter they will ever hear.

After hours of clinging to the crater wall, a cold rain begins to fall. Through the rain, Michael and Chris hear two voices from above.

It's too dangerous for us to attempt a rescue now.

You'll have to wait until tomorrow.

With toxic fumes burning their lungs, Michael and Chris must spend the night inside the volcano.

To make matters worse, the rain has soaked through their clothes. The men shiver as they struggle to hold on.

How are you doing, Chris?

I don't know if I can make it.

Just hold on. It's almost morning.

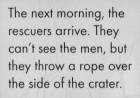

The next morning, the rescuers arrive. They can't see the men, but they throw a rope over the side of the crater.

I can't reach it!

The rescuers try again...

TO THE LEFT! TO THE LEFT!

WHOOSH!

...but the rope is still too far away for Michael to reach.

On the third try, the rope is only a few feet away. Michael prepares to jump when...

NO!

...the rope disappears again.

What's happening?

They pulled the rope away before I could grab it.

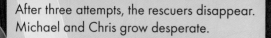

After three attempts, the rescuers disappear. Michael and Chris grow desperate.

I'm going to try to climb out!

I'm not gonna survive another night, Mike! I have to try.

Please be careful!

Are you sure, Chris? It's too dangerous.

Now Michael is completely alone. He tries to yell after Chris...

Chris! How are you doing up there?

...but he gets no reply.

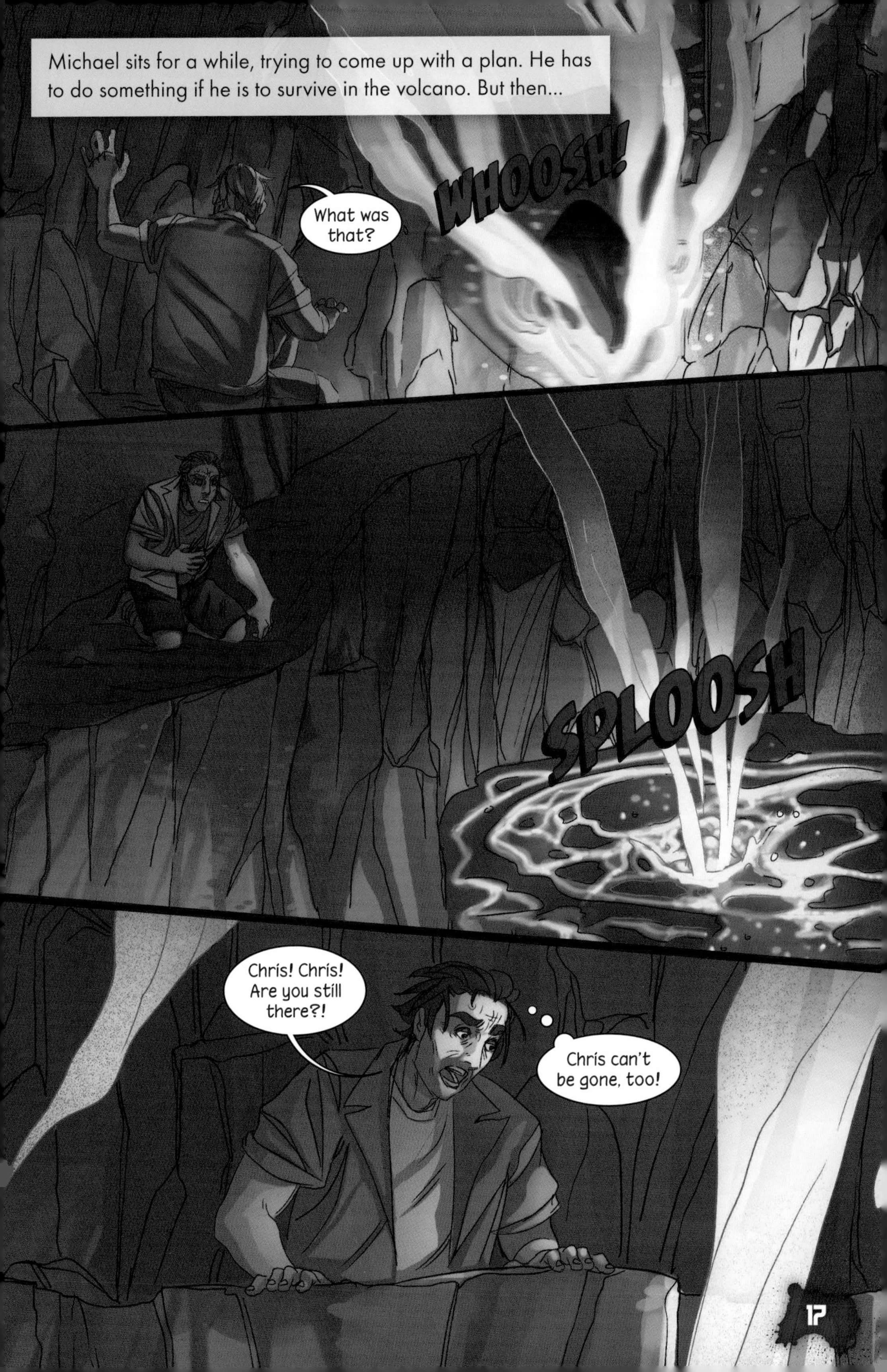

Michael sits for a while, trying to come up with a plan. He has to do something if he is to survive in the volcano. But then...
What was that?
WHOOSH!
SPLOOSH
Chris! Chris! Are you still there?!
Chris can't be gone, too!

RESCUED AT LAST

With Chris gone, the day passes slowly for Michael. As night falls, Michael realizes he has been in the volcano for more than 30 hours.

I probably don't have much time left.

Michael believes both of his friends are gone. He begins to give up hope that he will ever be rescued.

As the minutes slowly tick by, Michael imagines he sees the goddess Pele in the swirling smoke.

Pele, you might get me, too.

He passes his second night in the volcano with little rest.

The next morning, a helicopter swoops down into the smoke-filled crater.

Is he still alive?

The pilot does not have to wait long to get the answer to his question. Through the smoke, he sees Michael waving his arms.

Hey! I'm here. I'm here!

Stay there! I'll be right back.

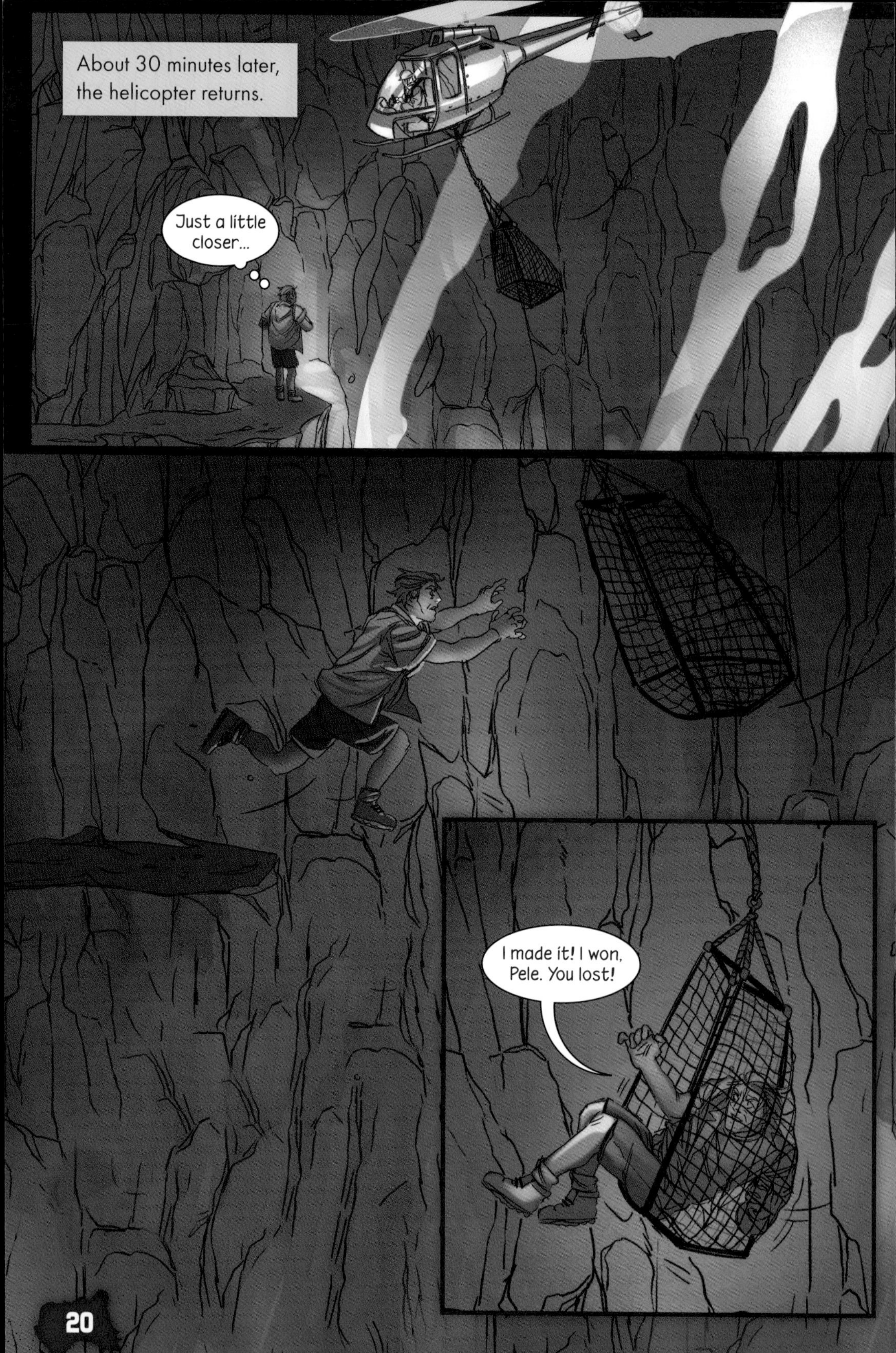
About 30 minutes later, the helicopter returns.
Just a little closer...
I made it! I won, Pele. You lost!

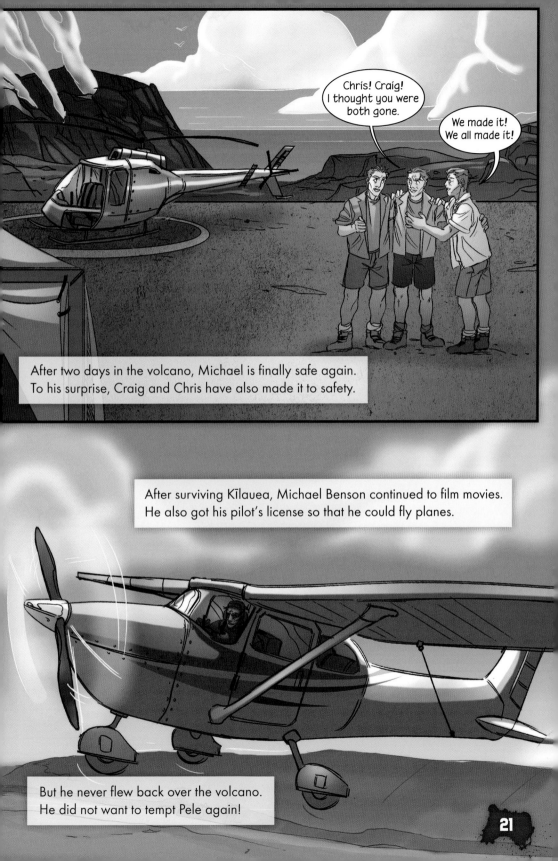

Chris! Craig! I thought you were both gone.

We made it! We all made it!

After two days in the volcano, Michael is finally safe again. To his surprise, Craig and Chris have also made it to safety.

After surviving Kīlauea, Michael Benson continued to film movies. He also got his pilot's license so that he could fly planes.

But he never flew back over the volcano. He did not want to tempt Pele again!

MORE ABOUT MICHAEL BENSON

+ The footage Michael filmed of the lava was destroyed in the crash.

+ Michael has filmed dozens of Hollywood movies, including the 2000 movie *X-Men* and the 2006 movie *Mission: Impossible III*.

+ After Craig fixed the radio battery, he was able to call for help. A helicopter pilot flew down into the crater to rescue him.

+ Chris managed to climb out of the crater. Then he found an empty rescue camp. Water and oxygen at the camp kept him alive until he was rescued by a helicopter.

+ After 35 years, the Pu'u 'Ō'ō crater stopped erupting in 2018.

MICHAEL BENSON TIMELINE

morning of November 21, 1992
Michael Benson, Chris Duddy, and Craig Hosking crash-land into the Kīlauea volcano

November 22, 1992
Chris manages to climb out of the volcano

afternoon of November 21, 1992
Craig is rescued by a helicopter

November 23, 1992
Michael is finally rescued by a helicopter

MICHAEL BENSON MAP

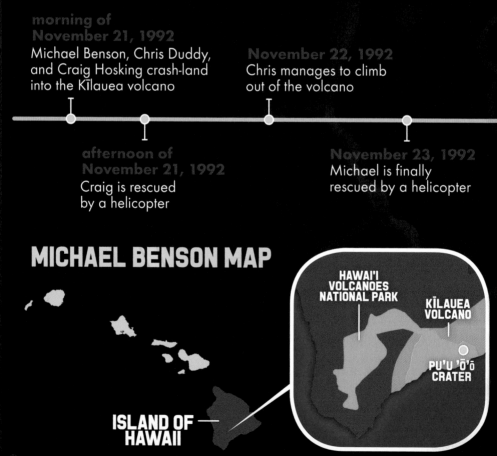

HAWAI'I VOLCANOES NATIONAL PARK

KĪLAUEA VOLCANO

PU'U 'Ō'ō CRATER

ISLAND OF HAWAII

GLOSSARY

crater—a large hole in the ground

footage—film recorded for television or movies

fumes—smoke or gases that are dangerous to breathe in

goddess—a female god

lava—extremely hot, fluid-like rock

legends—old stories that are passed down over time

mayday—a call for emergency help

molten—liquified due to extreme heat

toxic—poisonous

tradition—a custom, idea, or belief handed down over time

treacherous—very dangerous

TO LEARN MORE

AT THE LIBRARY

Berg, Shannon. *Hawaii Volcano of 2018*. Lake Elmo, Minn.: Focus Readers, 2020.

Hamalainen, Karina. *Hawai'i Volcanoes*. New York, N.Y.: Children's Press, 2019.

Loh-Hagan, Virginia. *Michael Benson: Trapped in a Volcano*. Ann Arbor, Mich.: Cherry Lake Publishing, 2019.

ON THE WEB

FACTSURFER

Factsurfer.com gives you a safe, fun way to find more information.

1. Go to www.factsurfer.com
2. Enter "Michael Benson" into the search box and click 🔍.
3. Select your book cover to see a list of related content.